A Note From the Designer

In our present world of "give me" or "I want more and bigger stuff," I don't really fit with my "Use it up, wear it out; fix it up or do without" philosophy of frugality. Five years ago, when our daughter asked if I would knit some clothes for her daughters' 18-inch dolls, I agreed readily, but the few patterns I found didn't meet my requirements. So I decided to design my own.

As you will find, my philosophy of frugality has carried over to my knitting obsession. My patterns knit up quickly, require a minimal number of same-size tools, and have few seams, thus saving you time as well as money. There are few closures to challenge small fingers, and you get the satisfaction of creating a unique garment that is attractive yet durable, serviceable and sure to please a small loved one. I hope you enjoy making these garments as much as I enjoyed designing them.

Jeanne

Jeanne Kussrow-Larson

Table of Contents

Belle of the Ball

Cooper catches everyone's eye wearing this evening gown with its matching shrug, dainty slippers and crocheted boa.

Skill Level

 INTERMEDIATE

Finished Measurements

Gown waist circumference: 11 inches
Gown length: Approx 13 inches
Shrug length: 2½ inches

Materials

- Caron Simply Soft Light (DK weight; 100% acrylic; 330 yds/85g per skein): 1 skein each pansy #0010 (A) and magenta #0011 (B)
- Patons Moxie (worsted weight; 100% polyester; 96 yds/100g per ball): 1 ball lynx #81008 (C)
- Size 2 (2.75mm) double-point needles (set of 4)
- Size 3 (3.25mm) double-point (set of 4) and 16-inch circular needle or size needed to obtain gauge
- Size 4 (3.5mm) 16-inch circular needle
- Size D/3 (3.25mm) crochet hook
- Size J/10 (6mm) crochet hook (for boa)
- Stitch markers
- Stitch holders (optional)
- 1 (½-inch) round shank button for shrug

3 LIGHT

4 MEDIUM

Gauge

30 sts and 40 rows/rnds = 4 inches/10cm in St st with size 3 needles.

To save time, take time to check gauge.

Special Abbreviations

Lifted Increase (LI): Knit into top of st (the purl bump) in the row below next st on LH needle.

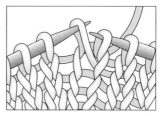

Lifted Increase

Wrap and Turn (W&T): Slip next st pwise to RH needle (Fig. 1). Bring yarn to RS of work between needles, then slip same st back to LH needle. Bring yarn to WS, wrapping st. Turn, leaving rem sts unworked, then beg working back in the other direction (Fig. 2). *To hide wraps on subsequent rows:* Work to wrapped st. With RH needle, pick up wrap and work wrap tog with wrapped st (Fig. 3).

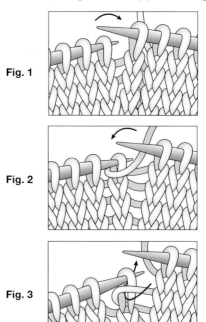

Fig. 1

Fig. 2

Fig. 3

Wrap and Turn

Pattern Stitches

Garter St (worked in rnds)
Rnd 1: Knit.

Rnd 2: Purl.

Rep Rnds 1 and 2 for pat.

Seed St
Rnd/Row 1: *K1, P1; rep from * to end.

Rnd/Row 2: Purl the knit sts and knit the purl sts.

Rep Rnd/Row 2 for pat.

Lace (multiple of 12 sts)
Rnd 1: *[K2tog] twice, [yo, k1] 3 times, yo, [ssk] twice, k1; rep from * around.

Rnd 2: Knit.

Rnd 3: Rep Rnd. 1.

Rnd 4: Knit.

Special Techniques

2- or 3-St I-Cord Bind-Off: Using knit cast-on method (see page 7), cast 2 (3) sts onto the LH needle; *k1 (2), ssk; do not turn; slip 2 (3) sts from RH needle to LH needle; rep from * until indicated number of sts have been bound off.

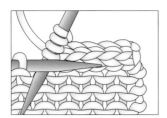

I-Cord Bind-Off

Provisional Cast-On: Using waste yarn and crochet hook, make a chain a few sts more than number of sts to be cast on. With knitting needle and project yarn, pick up and knit in back bump of each chain until required number of cast-on sts is on needle (Fig. 1). When indicated in pattern, "unzip" the crochet chain to free live sts (Fig. 2).

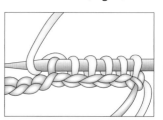

Fig. 1

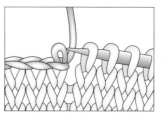

Fig. 2

Provisional Cast-On

Designer Tip

Here is an alternate way to work a Provisional Cast-On if you are not comfortable with crochet.

Waste Yarn/Crochet Thread Provisional Cast-On: *With waste yarn and dpn of required size, cast on required number of sts. Knit 1 rnd. Cut yarn. With crochet thread (size 3 works well), knit 1 rnd. Cut thread. With waste yarn, knit 1 more rnd. Cut yarn. Attach working yarn, leaving long tail, and begin project.*

To remove the waste yarn/crochet thread and rescue the "live" sts, pull the crochet thread firmly straight out to the side. When all the slack is pulled tight, the thread will slide out of the fabric. Peel away the first 2 rows of waste yarn stitches. Carefully slip the "live" sts onto knitting needle(s)—done more easily with a smaller needle than the size used to cast on—removing the waste yarn a stitch at a time.

Pattern Notes

The gown is worked in the round from the bottom to the underarm, at which point back and front are worked separately.

The shrug is worked back and forth from the top down; sleeves are completed in the round.

The slippers are worked in the round starting in the center of the sole; the sole stitches are grafted using Kitchener stitch (see page 6).

When working stripes, carry yarn not in use loosely up inside of piece, catching it periodically with other yarn.

When binding off, slip first stitch to be bound off.

Designer Tip

To splice a new yarn source of same color, just knit with the two yarns held together for two stitches. After working the stitches on the next round, tug on each yarn tail and the double yarn stitches will never be noticed. Weave in the two tails when doing your finishing chores.

Gown

Hem

With size 4 circular needle and A, cast on 120 sts; do not join.

Knit 3 rows; pm for beg of rnd and join, taking care not to twist sts.

Purling first rnd, work 6 rnds in garter st.

Skirt

With B, work 4-rnd Lace pat.

With A, knit 8 rnds; with B, work 4-rnd Lace pat.

With A, knit 7 rnds; with B, work Lace pat.

[With A, knit 6 rnds; with B, work Lace pat] twice.

Change to size 3 needle.

[With A, knit 5 rnds; with B, work Lace pat] twice.

With A, knit 4 rnds; with B, work Lace pat.

With A, knit 3 rnds; with B, work Lace pat.

With A, knit 3 rnds.

Waist

Change to size 3 dpns.

Dec rnd: With A, p2tog around—60 sts.

With B, work 6 rnds in Seed st.

Inc rnd: With B, *[LI, k1] 4 times, [LI, k2] 8 times; rep from * twice more—96 sts. Cut B.

With A, knit 5 rnds.

Back

Division row (RS): Divide back and front as follows: Firmly bind off 3 sts pwise, k45 (this includes the st on RH needle following bind-off); transfer last 48 sts to waste yarn for front—45 back sts rem.

Next row (WS): Firmly bind off 3 sts kwise, purl to end—42 sts.

Work 15 rows in St st.

Dec row: P5, p2tog, [p4, p2tog] 5 times, p5—36 sts.

Shape Back Neck

Division row (RS): K5; using 2-St I-Cord Bind-Off, bind off center 28 sts; k5 (including the 2 I-cord sts)—5 sts each side.

Next row (WS): P5; join 2nd ball of A, p5.

Working both sides at once with separate balls of yarn, work 9 rows in St st.

Cut yarns, leaving 12-inch tails.

Transfer sts to small safety pins as holders.

Front

Transfer 48 front sts to dpns.

Row 1 (RS): With A, firmly bind off 3 sts pwise, knit to end—45 sts.

Row 2: Firmly bind off 3 sts kwise, purl to end—42 sts.

Work 12 rows in St st.

Shape Armholes & V-Neck

Row 1 (RS): K21 sts for left front; join 2nd ball of yarn and k21 sts for right front.

Work both sides at once with separate balls of yarn.

Row 2: [P21] twice.

Dec row: K1, ssk, knit to 4 sts before neck opening, k2tog, k2; k2, ssk, knit to last 3 sts, k2tog, k1—19 sts each side.

Rep Dec row [every RS row] 3 more times—13 sts each side.

Dec at neck edges only [every RS row] 4 times, ending with a WS row—9 sts each side.

Knit to 6 sts before neck opening, [k2tog] twice, k2; k2, [ssk] twice, knit to end—5 sts each side after 2nd RS row.

Work 2 rows even.

Cut yarn, leaving 12-inch tails.

Pin the front and back straps tog, then try the dress on the doll to check the length. Knit a few more rows or rip some out as needed for fit.

Finishing

Graft front and back straps using Kitchener st.

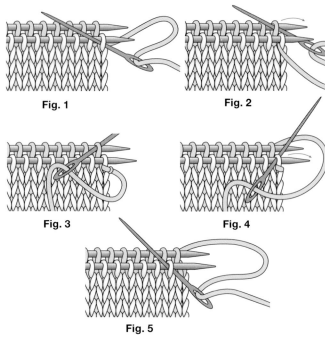

Fig. 1   **Fig. 2**

Fig. 3   **Fig. 4**

Fig. 5

Kitchener Stitch

Insert tapestry needle into first stitch on front needle as if to purl. Draw the yarn through, leaving stitch on needle (Fig 1). Insert tapestry needle into first stitch on back needle as if to purl. Slip stitch off the needle (Fig 2). Insert tapestry needle into next stitch on back needle as if to knit, leaving stitch on the needle; pull yarn through (Fig 3). Insert tapestry needle into first stitch on front needle as if to knit, and slip stitch off needle (Fig 4). Insert tapestry needle into next stitch on front needle as if to purl, leaving stitch on needle. Pull yarn through (Fig 5).

Tack the bottom of the V-neck closed using the tail at center V.

Sew the first few rows of hem closed.

Weave in all tails with tapestry needle.

Shrug

Body

With size 3 circular needle and B, cast on 67 sts; do not join.

Set-up row (RS): Work in Seed st, placing markers as follows: Work 10 front sts, pm, work 13 sleeve sts, pm, work 21 back sts, pm, work 13 sleeve sts, pm, work 10 front sts.

Buttonloop row: Continuing in Seed st, work to last st; using the Knitted Cast-On, cast on 8 sts for button loop, turn; sl 1, bind off next 6 sts—2 sts rem on RH needle. Pass both sts back to LH needle and k3tog-tbl to form a buttonloop.

Work 2 rows in Seed st.

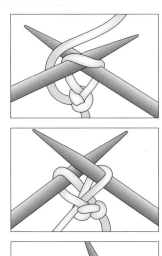

Knitted Cast-On

Knit a stitch into the loop and place it on the left needle. Repeat until you have cast on the number of stitches indicated in the pattern.

Raglan Inc row (RS): Work 5 sts in Seed st for band, [knit to 1 st before marker, yo, k1, sm, k1, yo] 4 times, knit to last 5 sts, work 5 sts in Seed st for band—75 sts.

Next row: Work 5 band sts in Seed st, purl to 2nd marker, [p5, kfb] 4 times; purl to last 5 sts, work band sts in Seed st—79 sts.

Maintaining band sts in Seed st and all other sts in St st, rep Raglan Inc row on next row, then [every RS row] 3 more times—111 sts.

Raglan Inc/Front Dec row: Work 5 band sts, ssk, [knit to 1 st before marker, yo, k1, sm, k1, yo] 4 times, knit to last 7 sts, k2tog, work 5 band sts—117 sts.

Rep Raglan Inc/Front Dec row [every RS row] 4 more times—141 sts, with 15 sts each front, 33 sts each sleeve and 45 back sts.

Division row (WS): Removing all markers, [work Seed st to marker; transfer 33 sleeve sts to waste yarn] twice, work Seed st to end—75 body sts.

Edging

Maintaining established Seed st, dec 1 st each end [every RS row] 3 times—69 sts.

Last row (WS): Slipping first st, bind off kwise until 1 st rem on LH needle, slip st on RH needle back to LH needle, pass 2nd st over first st. Cut yarn and fasten off last st.

Sleeves

Transfer 33 sleeve sts to 3 size 3 dpns; mark beg of rnd and join.

Work 3 rnds in Seed st.

Bind off pwise.

Finishing

Use tails to close any holes at underarm.

Weave in all ends.

Sew button to left front opposite button loop.

Slippers

Leaving a 15-inch tail, using size 2 dpns, Provisional Cast-On and B, cast on 35 sts; divide sts as follows: 11, 14, 10; mark beg of rnd and join, taking care not to twist sts

Rnd 1: Purl around.

Rnd 2: P3, LI, p14, LI, p1, LI, p14, LI, p3—39 sts.

Rnd 3 (with short rows): P28, W&T; k8, LI, k1, LI, k8, W&T; purl to end, hiding wrap when you come to it—41 sts.

Rnd 4: P3, LI, p16, LI, p3, LI, p16, LI, p3, hiding wrap when you come to it—45 sts.

Rnd 5: Purl around.

Rnd 6: P3, LI, p17, LI, p5, LI, p17, LI, p3—49 sts.

Knit 2 rnds.

Shape Toe

Rnd 1: K19, ssk, k7, k2tog, k19—47 sts.

Rnds 2, 4 and 6: Knit around.

Rnd 3: K19, ssk, k5, k2tog, k19—45 sts.

Rnd 5: K19, ssk, k3, k2tog, k19—43 sts.

Rnd 7: K18, ssk, sk2p, k2tog, k18—39 sts.

Rnd 8: K18, sk2p, k18—37 sts.

Using 3-St I-Cord Bind-Off, bind off all sts.

Cut yarn and pull tail through the rem 3 I-cord sts.

Finishing

Unzip Provisional Cast-On, placing 35 live sts evenly divided on 2 smaller dpns.

Close bottom by grafting sts tog using cast-on tail and Kitchener st.

Weave in all ends.

Designer Tip

When dressing an 18-Inch doll with the knit dresses or sweaters found in this book, the following method is recommended. Put both of her hands up (as if reaching for the sky). Bring the garment over her head and pull it down so the neck hole covers her eyes. Gently pull the body of the garment away from her head and put the right (or left) arm in the armhole. Don't pull the garment down yet. Do the same with the other arm. Now pull the garment down the arms and head, down to the neck. Put her arms down and settle the garment into place.

Boa

With larger crochet hook and D, make chain approx 36 inches long.

Chain Stitch

Work dc in 4th ch from hook, *ch 1, skip next ch, dc in next ch; rep from * to end.

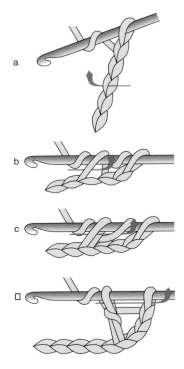

a

b

c

▯

Double Crochet

Cut yarn and fasten off. Weave in ends.

To fluff up the boa, use a knitting needle to "pick" and "brush" the yarn that gets caught in the sts. ●

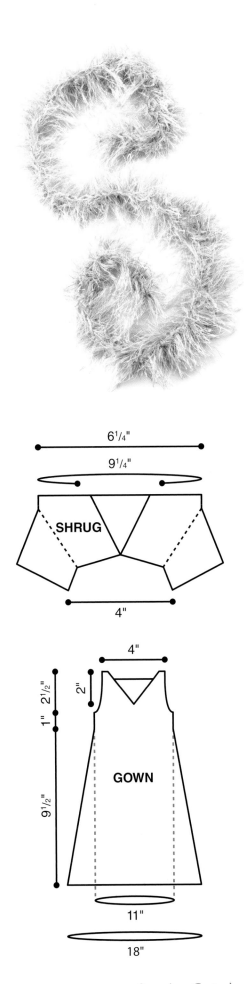

6¼"

9¼"

SHRUG

4"

4"

2"

1" 2½"

9½"

GOWN

11"

18"

Spring Is Here

Gentle raindrops are welcomed by Lizabeth in her lacy
spring dress with matching hat, socks and mesh bag.

Skill Level

■■□□ EASY

Finished Measurements

Dress waist circumference: 11 inches
Dress length: Approx 9½ inches
Hat circumference: Approx 10 inches

Materials

- Caron Simply Soft Light
  (DK weight; 100% acrylic;
  330 yds/85g per skein): 1 skein
  each key lime #0005 (A) and bubble gum
  #0012 (B)
- Size 2 (2.75mm) double-point needles
- Size 3 (3.25mm) 16-inch circular and double-point needles or size needed to obtain gauge
- Size D/3 (3.25mm) crochet hook
- Small stitch holders or large safety pins
- Stitch markers
- 3 (⅝-inch) flower buttons for dress and bag
- 2 (½-inch) flower buttons for shoes (optional)

Gauge

30 sts and 40 rnds = 4 inches/10cm in Dots pat with
larger needles.

To save time, take time to check gauge.

Special Abbreviations

Lifted Increase (LI): Knit into top of st (the purl
bump) in the row below next st on LH needle
(see page 2).

Pattern Stitches

Seed St (even number of sts)
Row/Rnd 1: *K1, p1; rep from * around.

Row/Rnd 2: Knit the purl sts and purl the knit sts.

Rep Row/Rnd 2 for pat.

Dots (multiple of 4 sts, worked in rnds)
*Note: A chart is provided for those preferring to work Dots
pat from a chart.*

Rnd 1: *K3, p1; rep from * around.

Rnd 2: Knit.

Rnd 3: *K1, p1, k2; rep from * around.

Rnd 4: Knit.

Rep Rnds 1–4 for pat.

Dots (multiple of 4 sts, worked in rows)
Row 1 (RS): *K3, p1; rep from * to end.

Row 2: Purl.

Row 3: K1, p1, *k3, p1; rep from * to last 2 sts, k2.

Row 4: Purl.

Rep Rows 1–4 for pat.

Lace (multiple of 8 sts)

Note: A chart is provided for those preferring to work Lace pat from a chart.

Rnd 1: *K2, [yo, k2tog] twice, k2; rep from * around.

Rnd 2 and all even-numbered rnds: Knit.

Rnd 3: *K1, yo, k2tog, k1; rep from * around.

Rnd 5: *Yo, k2tog, k4, yo, k2tog; rep from * around.

Rnd 7: Rep Rnd 3.

Rnd 8: Knit.

Rep Rnds 1–8 for pat.

Faggoting (even number of sts)
Rnd 1: *K2tog, yo; rep from * around.

Rnd 2: Knit.

Rep Rnds 1 and 2 for pat.

Special Techniques
2-St I-Cord Bind-Off: *K1, ssk, sl 2 sts back to LH needle; rep from * until indicated number of sts have been bound off (see page 4).

2- or 3-St I-Cord: *K2 (3), slip sts back to LH needle; rep from * until cord is desired length.

I-Cord: Using dpn and backward-loop method, cast on desired number of sts. Knit across; do not turn. Slide sts to opposite end of dpn. Pulling working yarn tightly across back of piece, knit across; do not turn. Rep until I-cord measures desired length. Bind off, then cut yarn and pull end through sts.

Provisional Cast-On: Using waste yarn and crochet hook, make a chain a few sts more than the number of sts to be cast on. With knitting needle and project yarn, pick up and knit in back bump of each chain until required number of cast-on sts is on needle. When indicated in pattern, "unzip" the crochet chain to free live sts and transfer them to smaller dpns (see page 4).

Pattern Notes
Dress is worked in the round from the bottom to the underarms, at which point the front and back are worked separately; shoulder seams are joined using Kitchener stitch (see page 6).

The hat is worked in the round from lower ruffle to crown.

Shoes and socks are worked in the round starting in the center of the sole; the sole stitches are grafted using Kitchener stitch.

When binding off, slip first st to be bound off.

Dress

Skirt
With larger circular needle and A, cast on 120 sts. Do not join.

> ## Designer Tip
>
> *As you work the 120-stitch cast-on, place a stitch marker after every 20 stitches to keep track of the number of stitches on the needle; use a contrasting-color marker to indicate the beginning of the round. Remove markers when no longer needed.*

Work 3 rows in Seed st; at end of Row 3, pm for beg of rnd and join.

Work 3 rnds in established Seed st.

Work [Rnds 1–8 of Lace pat] 5 times.

Work Rnds 1–4 of Lace pat.

Knit 4 rnds.

Shape Waist

Change to larger dpns.

Dec rnd: [K2tog] around—60 sts. Do not cut A; carry up inside of piece.

Join B and knit 1 rnd.

Work 3 rnds Seed st.

Change to smaller dpns; work 3 rnds Seed st.

Change to larger dpns; work 1 rnd Seed st.

Inc rnd: *[M1, k1] 4 times, [M1, k2] 8 times; rep from * twice more; cut B—96 sts.

Bodice

With A, knit 1 rnd.

Work 4-rnd Dots pat.

Division row: Slipping first st, bind off 2 sts pwise; work 46 sts (including st on RH needle following bind-off) in established pat; transfer rem 48 sts to holder for front—46 back sts rem.

Back

Next row (WS): Slipping first st, bind off 2 sts kwise, purl to end—44 sts.

Set-up row (RS): P2, work in established pat to last 2 sts, p2.

Purling first and last 2 sts of each row, work 21 rows in established Dots pat, ending with a WS row.

Back Neck

Division row (RS): Work 16 sts in established pat; kfb, then slip those 2 sts back to LH needle; work 2-St I-Cord Bind-Off across center 13 sts; work 16 sts in established pat to end—16 sts each side.

Next row: P16; on other side of opening, insert LH needle into first st on inner side of I-cord; join new ball of yarn and purl picked-up st tog with first st on LH needle; insert LH needle into first st on outer side of I-cord, then purl picked-up st tog with next st on LH needle; purl to end of row.

Dec row (RS): Working both sides at once with separate balls of yarn, work in established pat to 4 sts before neck opening, k2tog, k2; k2 ssk, work in pat to end—15 sts each side.

Maintaining 2 sts each side of neck in St st and rest of sts in established pat, rep Dec row on next RS row, then work 5 rows even—14 sts each side.

Transfer each set of shoulder sts to separate holder or large safety pin.

Cut yarns, leaving 15-inch tails.

Front

Transfer 48 front sts to larger dpn; join A and maintaining established pat, bind off 2 sts at beg of next 2 rows—44 sts.

Purling first and last 2 sts of each row, work 16 rows in established Dots pat, ending with a WS row.

Front Neck

Division row (RS): Work 17 sts in established pat; kfb, then slip the 2 inc sts back to LH needle; work 2-St I-Cord Bind-Off across center 11 sts; work 17 sts in established pat to end—17 sts each side.

Next row (WS): P17; on other side of opening, insert LH needle into first st on inner side of I-cord; join new ball of yarn and purl picked-up st tog with first st on LH needle; insert LH needle into first st on outer side of I-cord, then purl picked-up st tog with next st on LH needle; purl to end of row.

Dec row (RS): Work in established pat to 4 sts before neck, k2tog, k2; k2, ssk, work in pat to end—16 sts each side.

Maintaining pat, rep Dec row [every RS row] twice more—14 sts each side.

Work 8 rows even, ending with a RS row.

Cut yarns, leaving 15-inch tails.

Finishing

Transfer front and back left shoulder sts to 2 dpns.

Graft shoulder sts using Kitchener st.

Rep for right shoulder.

Using cast-on tail, sew edges first few rows tog.

Sew 2 buttons to center front above waistband.

Hat

Ruffle

Note: *Change to dpns when sts no longer fit comfortably on circular needle.*

With larger circular needle and A, cast on 128 sts. Pm for beg of rnd and join, taking care not to twist sts.

Rnds 1–3: *P3, k5; rep from * around.

Rnd 4: *P2tog, p1, k5; rep from * around—112 sts.

Rnds 5 and 6: *P2, k5; rep from * around.

Rnd 7: *P2tog, k5; rep from * around—96 sts.

Rnd 8: *P1, k5; rep from * around.

Rnd 9: *K2tog, k4; rep from * around—80 sts.

Rnd 10: Knit and dec 9 sts evenly spaced around—71 sts.

Do not cut A; carry loosely up inside of hat, catching with B every few rnds to secure.

Band
Join B; work 9 rnds in Seed st. Cut B.

Body
Rnd 1: With A, k2tog, knit to end—70 sts.

Knit 25 rnds.

Next rnd: *K5, pm; rep from * around.

Shape Crown
Dec rnd: *Knit to 2 sts before marker, k2tog; rep from * around—56 sts.

Rep Dec rnd [every other rnd] 3 more times—14 sts.

Last rnd: K2tog around—7 sts.

"Button" Bobble
Place rem 7 sts on 1 dpn.

Row 1 (RS): K2tog, k4, do not turn—6 sts, with 5 on RH needle and 1 on LH needle.

Row 2 (RS): Slip 5 sts on RH needle to LH needle; k5, then pass the 2nd, 3rd, 4th and 5th sts on RH needle over the first st; do not turn—1 st rem on each needle.

Row 3 (RS): Slip the st on RH needle to LH needle; k2tog-tbl.

Cut yarn, leaving a 12-inch tail. Fasten off last st.

Tack "button" to top of hat.

Weave in all ends.

Lacy Socks

Note: *Commercial doll shoes will not fit over these socks. The Mary Jane shoes that follow will stretch over the socks.*

Leaving a 15-inch tail, using smaller dpns, Provisional Cast-On and A, cast on 34 sts. Divide sts on 3 dpns as follows: 9, 14, 9; mark beg of rnd and join, taking care not to twist sts.

Rnds 1, 3, 5 and 7: Knit around.

Rnd 2: K2, LI, k12, LI, k4, LI, k12, LI, k2—36 sts.

Rnd 4: K4, LI, k12, LI, k4, LI, k12, LI, k4—40 sts.

Rnd 6: K3, LI, k15, LI, k4, LI, k15, LI, k3—44 sts.

Rnd 8: K19, pm, k6, pm, k19.

Dec rnd: Slipping markers when you come to them, knit to 2 sts before marker, ssk, knit to next marker, k2tog, knit to end of rnd—42 sts.

Continuing in St st, rep Dec rnd [every other rnd] 5 more times—32 sts.

Knit 1 rnd.

Next rnd: Removing markers, k6, [k2tog] 3 times, k8, [k2tog] 3 times; k6—26 sts.

Knit 2 rnds.

Inc rnd: [K6, LI] 4 times, k2—30 sts.

Knit 2 rnds, adjusting sts on dpns (if necessary) so that there are 10 sts on each dpn.

Work 8 rnds of Faggotting pat.

Bind off pwise.

Cut yarn, leaving 8-inch tail.

Finishing

Unzip Provisional Cast-On, placing 32 live sts evenly divided on 2 smaller dpns.

Close bottom by grafting sts tog using Kitchener st.

Weave in all tails.

Mary Jane Shoes

Leaving a 15-inch tail, using larger dpns, Provisional Cast-On and B, cast on 34 sts. Divide sts on 3 dpns as follows: 10, 14, 10; mark beg of rnd and join, taking care not to twist sts

Rnds 1, 3, 5, 7, 8 and 9: Knit.

Rnd 2: K3, LI, k11, LI, k6, LI, k11, LI, k3—38 sts.

Rnd 4: K3, LI, k13, LI, k6, LI, k13, LI, k3—42 sts.

Rnd 6: K3, LI, k15, LI, k6, LI, k15, LI, k3—46 sts.

Rnd 10: K19, pm, k8, pm, k19.

Rnd 11: Slipping markers when you come to them, knit to 2 sts before marker, ssk, knit to next marker, k2tog, knit to end of rnd—44 sts.

Rnd 12: Rep Rnd 11—42 sts.

Rnd 13: Knit to 4 sts before marker, k2tog, ssk, k8, k2tog twice; knit to end of rnd—38 sts.

Rnd 14: Removing markers when you come to them, k9; bind off 17 sts; kfb, k1 (there are 4 sts on RH needle and 9 sts on LH needle); slip the 4 sts to a large safety pin for strap; knit to end of rnd, then k9 to opening—18 sts.

Turn and bind off all sts kwise; do not fasten off last st and do not cut yarn—1 st rem on RH needle.

Strap

Slide the st on RH needle and the 4 sts from safety pin to smaller dpn—5 sts on dpn.

With WS facing and using smaller dpns, p2tog, p1, p2tog; turn—3 sts on dpn.

Work 3-St I-Cord for 2¼ inches.

Cut yarn, leaving 8-inch tail.

Using tapestry needle, thread tail through rem sts and pull tight.

Sew end of strap to other side of shoe.

Optional: Sew 2 small buttons to shoes' outer sides at strap level to indicate left and right shoes.

Finishing

Unzip Provisional Cast-On, placing 34 live sts evenly divided on 2 smaller dpns.

Close bottom by grafting sts tog using Kitchener st.

Weave in all tails.

Mesh Bag

Leaving a 15-inch tail and using Provisional Cast-On, larger dpns and B, cast on 22 sts; mark beg of rnd and join, taking care not to twist sts.

Rnds 1, 3 and 5: Knit around.

Rnd 2: K6, LI, k6, LI, k6, LI, k1—25 sts.

Rnd 4: [K3, LI] 7 times, k4—32 sts.

Purl 2 rnds; cut B, leaving 8-inch tail.

Join A; knit 1 rnd, adjusting sts on dpns as necessary so that each dpn has an even number of sts.

Work 10 rnds of Faggoting pat.

Bind off all sts pwise.

Handle

Work 2-St I-Cord for 5 inches.

Sew ends to sides of bag (see photo).

Sew on button.

Finishing

Unzip Provisional Cast-On, placing 22 live sts evenly divided on 2 smaller dpns.

Close bottom by grafting sts tog using Kitchener st. ●

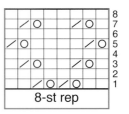

LACE PAT CHART

STITCH KEY	
□	K
O	Yo
╱	K2tog

DOTS PAT CHART

STITCH KEY	
□	K on RS, p on WS
−	P on RS, k on WS

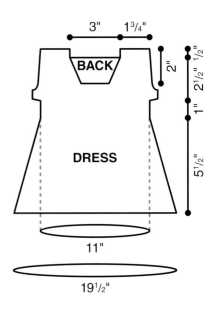

BACK

3" 1¾" 2" ½" 2½" ½" 1"

DRESS

5½"

11"

19½"

Summer Fun

Caiden is ready for warm summer weather in her gored skirt and adorable tank top; her matching accessories are perfect for cooler evenings or air-conditioned buildings.

Skill Level

■■■□ INTERMEDIATE

Finished Measurements

Cardigan chest: 12 inches (buttoned)
Cardigan length: 5 inches
Tank top chest: 10½ inches
Tank top length: 5½ inches
Skirt length: 6 inches

Materials

- Caron Simply Soft Light (DK weight; 100% acrylic; 330 yds/85g per skein): 1 skein each Riviera #0008 (A), heavy cream #0002 (B) and real red #0013 (C)
- Size 2 (2.75mm) double-point needles (set of 4)
- Size 3 (3.25mm) double-point (set of 4) and 16-inch circular needles or size needed to obtain gauge
- Size 4 (3.5mm) double-point needles (set of 4)
- Size D/3 (3.25mm) crochet hook
- Stitch holders or 2 large safety pins
- Stitch markers in 2 colors (A and B)
- 5 (⅜-inch) shank buttons

3 LIGHT

Gauge

30 sts and 40 rnds/rows = 4 inches/10cm in St st with size 3 needles.

To save time, take time to check gauge.

Special Abbreviations

Place marker A, place marker B (pmA, pmB): Place marker A on needle, place marker B on needle.

Slip marker (sm): Slip marker from LH to RH needle.

Lifted Increase (LI): Knit into top of st (the purl bump) in the row below next st on LH needle (see page 2).

Lifted Increase-Purl (LI-P): Purl into top of st (the purl bump) in the row below next st on LH needle.

Knit in front, back and front of st (kfbf): Knit in front, back and front of st to inc 2 sts.

Slip, slip, purl (ssp): Slip 2 sts 1 at a time kwise to RH needle; return sts to LH needle in turned position and p2tog-tbl—a left-leaning single dec.

Tuck 1 (T1): Insert RH needle into st in Rnd 1 below the next st on LH needle and draw up a loop; knit next st on LH needle, then pass the loop over the st just knitted.

Pattern Stitches

Seed St
Rnd/Row 1: K1, p1 around/across.

Rnd/Row 2: Purl the knit sts and knit the purl sts.

Rep Rnd/Row 2 for pat.

Garter St
Rnd 1: Knit.

Rnd 2: Purl.

Rep Rnds 1 and 2 for pat.

Stripe
Working in St st, work 4 rows C, [work 2 rows A, work 4 rows C] twice.

Special Techniques

2- or 3-St I-Cord: Cast on 2 (3) sts; *k3, do not turn; slip sts back to LH needle; rep from * until cord is desired length.

3-St I-Cord Bind-Off: *K2, ssk; sl 3 sts back to LH needle; rep from * until indicated number of sts have been bound off (see page 4).

Provisional Cast-On: Using waste yarn and crochet hook, make a chain a few sts more than the number of sts to be cast on. With knitting needle and project yarn, pick up and knit in back bump of each chain until required number of cast-on sts is on needle. When indicated in pattern, "unzip" the crochet chain to free live sts (see page 4).

Intarsia: Work the different colors using separate sources of yarn—do not carry yarn that is not in use across back. If desired, wind yarns on separate yarn bobbins or make butterflies. At color change, bring the new color from below the color just used to twist them together and prevent holes.

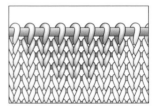 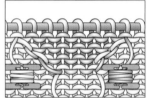

Intarsia

Pattern Notes
The raglan cardigan is worked in one piece from the top down. Bands are worked entirely with A, so when working striped rows with C, use a separate ball of A for bands as necessary, working as for intarsia.

The tank top is worked in the round from the bottom to the underarms, after which the front and back are worked separately; waist is shaped by changing needle sizes.

The skirt is worked in the round from the waist down and has faux seams made with slipped stitches.

Shoes and socks are worked in the round starting in the center of the sole; the sole stitches are grafted using Kitchener stitch (see page 6).

When binding off, slip first stitch to be bound off.

Cardigan

Yoke

With size 3 circular needle and A, cast on 68 sts; do not join.

Work 2 rows in Seed st.

Set-up row (RS): Work across in established Seed st, placing markers as follows: 5 front band sts, pmA, 7 front sts, pmB, 12 sleeve sts, pmB, 20 back sts, pmB, 12 sleeve sts, pmB, 7 front sts, pmA, 5 front band sts.

Buttonhole row (WS): K1, p2tog, yo (first buttonhole), work Seed st to end. *Note: Work buttonhole in right front band [every 8 rows] 4 more times.*

Raglan Inc row (RS): Work 8 raglan incs as follows: Work 5-st band in Seed st, [knit to 1 st before marker B, LI, k1, sm, LI] 4 times, knit to last 5 sts, work 5-st band in Seed st—76 sts.

Next 7 rows: Working band sts in Seed st and all other sts in St st with A, rep Raglan Inc row [every RS row] 3 more times, ending with a WS row (also a Buttonhole row)—100 sts.

Next row (RS): Beg Stripe pat as follows: Work 5 band sts with A; join C, and working raglan incs at B markers as before, knit to Marker A; join 2nd small ball of A and work 5 band sts in Seed st—108 sts.

Next 15 rows: Maintaining bands in A and continuing to make buttonholes every 8 rows, work sts between A markers in Stripe pat, and *at the same time*, con-tinue working Raglan inc row [every RS row] 7 times, ending with a WS row (also a Buttonhole row). Cut C—164 sts.

Last raglan row: Working with A only, rep Raglan Inc row—172 sts, with 5 band sts each side, 20 sts each front, 38 sts each sleeve and 46 back sts.

Division row (WS): Removing B markers when you come to them, work 5 band sts, *purl to 2 sts before marker B, LI-P, p1, sl 1; transfer next 38 sts to waste yarn for sleeve; pass the slipped st from RH needle to LH needle; purl the slipped st and next st on LH needle tog (this helps tighten underarm gap); rep from * once, purl to last 5 sts, work 5 band sts— 96 body sts.

Body

Maintaining 5 band sts each side in Seed st, work 11 rows in St st, remembering to work last Buttonhole row.

Removing A markers, work 5 rows in Seed st.

Bind off in pat.

Cut yarn, leaving an 8-inch tail.

Sleeve

Transfer 38 sleeve sts from waste yarn to 3 size 3 dpns; mark beg of rnd.

Join A; work in Seed st around, then pick up and knit 2 sts from body underarm—40 sts.

Work 3 rnds in Seed st.

Bind off pwise.

Cut yarn, leaving 8-inch tail.

Finishing

Weave in tails.

Sew 5 buttons to left front band, aligned with buttonholes.

Tank Top

With size 4 dpns and B, cast on 88 sts; divide sts on 3 dpns as follows: 32, 28, 28; mark beg of rnd and join, taking care not to twist sts.

Rnds 1–10: *P1, k3; rep from * around.

Rnds 11–17: Change to size 2 dpns; *k1, p3; rep from * around.

Rnds 18–26: Change to size 3 dpns; work in established pat.

Division row (RS): Bind off 2 sts, k3 (including st on RH needle from bind-off), [p3, k1] 9 times, k3; slip next 44 sts to holder for front—42 sts rem for back.

Back

Next row (WS): Bind off 1 st, work in established pat to last 2 sts, k2—41 sts.

Knitting first and last 2 sts of each row, work 16 rows even.

Shape Back Neck

Next row (RS): Work 12 sts in established pat; kfbf, slip the last 3 sts worked to LH needle; work 3-St I-Cord Bind-Off across center 19 sts (12 sts rem on LH needle, including the 3 I-cord sts); work in established pat to end—12 sts rem each side.

Designer Tip

Cast-on tail in the way? Tie a bow in one tail or tie two or more tails together to keep them out of the way so you don't begin working the pattern with a tail instead of the working yarn!

Next row (WS): Working both sides at once with separate balls of yarn, work in established pat to neck opening; on other side of opening, insert LH needle into first st on inner side of I-cord; join new ball of yarn and purl picked-up st tog with first st on LH needle; insert LH needle into first st on outer side of I-cord, then purl picked-up st tog with next st on LH needle; work in established pat to end—12 sts each side.

Dec row (RS): Maintaining established pat, work to 4 sts before neck edge, k2tog; k2; k2, ssk, work in established pat to end—11 sts each side.

Rep Dec row [every RS row] 3 times—8 sts each side.

Work 2 rows even.

Transfer shoulder sts to separate large safety pins. Cut yarns, leaving 15-inch tails.

Front

Transfer 44 front sts from holder to size 3 dpn.

With RS facing, rejoin yarn; maintaining pat, bind off 2 sts at beg of next row, then 1 st at beg of following row—41 sts.

Knitting first and last 2 sts of each row for armhole edge, work 5 rows even.

Next row (WS): Work 20 sts in established pat, LI, work in pat to end—42 sts.

Next row: K3, [p3, k1] 4 times, k4, [k1, p3] 4 times, k3.

Next row: K2, [p1, k3] 4 times, p6, [k3, p1] 4 times, k2.

Shape Front Neck

Row 1 (RS): Maintaining armhole edges in garter st, work 17 sts in established pat, k2tog, k2; leaving an 8-inch tail, join 2nd ball of yarn; k2, ssk, work in pat to end—20 sts each side.

Row 2: Working both sides at once with separate balls of yarn, work even.

Dec row (RS): Work to 4 sts before neck edge, k2tog, k2; k2, ssk, work in pat to end—19 sts each side.

Rep Dec row [every RS row] 3 times—16 sts each side.

Dec row (WS): Work to 4 sts before neck edge, ssp, p2; p2, p2tog, work in pat to end—15 sts each side.

Continue to dec at neck edge [every row] 7 more times—8 sts each side.

Work 2 rows even.

Cut yarns, leaving 15-inch tails for shoulder seams.

Finishing

Transfer left back shoulder sts to dpn. Join front and back left shoulder sts using Kitchener st (see page 6).

Rep for right shoulder.

Use tail at center front neck to tack the V so it doesn't gap too much.

Weave in ends.

Skirt

Note: Change to circular needle when there are enough sts to fit around.

With size 3 dpn and A, cast on 56 sts; divide sts among 3 dpns; mark beg of rnd and join, taking care not to twist sts.

Rnds 1–4: Work in 1x1 Rib.

Rnd 5 (Eyelet rnd): K5, yo, k2tog, [k4, yo, k2tog] 7 times, k7.

Rnd 6: Work in 1x1 Rib.

Rnd 7: K5, [pm, sl 1, k6] 7 times, pm, sl 1, k1.

Rnd 8 and all even-numbered rnds: Knit around.

Rnd 9: [Knit to marker, sm, sl 1] 8 times, knit to end of rnd.

Rnd 11 (inc): [Knit to 1 st before marker, LI, k1, sm, sl 1, LI] 8 times; knit to end of rnd—72 sts.

Rnds 13 and 15: [Knit to marker, sm, sl 1] 8 times, knit to end of rnd.

Rnd 17: Rep Rnd 11—88 sts.

Rnds 19 and 21: Rep Rnd 9.

Rnd 23: Rep Rnd 11—104 sts.

Rnds 25, 27, 29 and 31: Rep Rnd 9.

Rnd 33: Rep Rnd 11—120 sts.

Rnds 35, 37, 39, 41, 43, 45, 47, 49 and 51: Rep Rnd 9.

Rnd 53: [Knit to 1 st before marker, LI, k1, sm, sl 1] 8 times, knit to end of rnd—128 sts.

Rnds 55, 57 and 59: Rep Rnd 9.

Lower Edge

Next rnd: Removing markers, k2tog, work in Seed st to end of rnd—127 sts.

Work 5 rnds in Seed st.

Bind off pwise.

Cut yarn leaving an 8-inch tail.

Finishing

Weave in all ends.

Belt

With size 2 dpns and C, cast on 2 sts.

Work 2-St I-Cord for approx 26 inches.

Weave belt through holes of Eyelet rnd on skirt, then tie in bow.

Socks

Note: Commercial doll shoes will not fit over these socks; the T-strap sandals that follow will stretch over the socks.

Leaving a 15-inch tail, using Provisional Cast-On, size 2 dpn and B, cast on 32 sts; divide sts on 3 dpns as follows: 9, 14, 9; mark beg of rnd and join, taking care not to twist sts.

Rnds 1, 3, 5 and 7: Knit around.

Rnd 2: K2, LI, k12, LI, k4, LI, k12, LI, k2—36 sts.

Rnd 4: K4, LI, k12, LI, k4, LI, k12, LI, k4—40 sts.

Rnd 6: K3, LI, k15, LI, k4, LI, k15, LI, k3—44 sts.

Rnd 8: K19, pm, k6, pm, k19.

Dec rnd: Knit to 2 sts before marker, ssk, knit to marker, k2tog; knit to end of rnd—42 sts.

Rep Dec rnd [every other rnd] 5 more times, ending with a non-dec rnd—32 sts.

Next rnd: Removing markers, k6, [k2tog] 3 times, k8, [k2tog] 3 times, k6—26 sts.

Knit 2 rnds.

Inc rnd: [K3, LI] 8 times, k2—34 sts.

Work 4 rnds in 1x1 Rib.

With A, knit 1 rnd.

Work 1 rnd in 1x1 Rib; cut A, leaving an 8-inch tail.

With B, knit 1 rnd.

Work 1 rnd in 1x1 Rib.

With C, knit 1 rnd.

Work 1 rnd in 1x1 Rib; cut C, leaving an 8-inch tail.

With B, knit 1 rnd.

Work 2 rnds in 1x1 Rib.

Bind off loosely in rib. Cut B, leaving an 8-inch tail.

Finishing

Unzip Provisional Cast-On, placing 32 live sts evenly divided on 2 smaller dpns.

Close bottom by grafting sts tog using cast-on tail and Kitchener st.

Weave in all ends.

T-Strap Sandals

Leaving a 15-inch tail, using Provisional Cast-On, size 3 dpn and C, cast on 34 sts; divide sts on 3 dpns as follows: 10, 14, 10; mark beg of rnd and join, taking care not to twist sts.

Rnds 1, 3 and 5: Knit around.

Rnd 2: K3, LI, k11, LI, k6, LI, k11, LI, k3—38 sts.

Rnd 4: K3, LI, k13, LI, k6, LI, k13, LI, k3—42 sts.

Rnd 6: K3, LI, k14, LI, k1, [yo, k2tog] twice, k2, LI, k15, LI, k3—46 sts.

Rnd 7: K19, pm, [k2tog, yo] 4 times, k19.

Rnd 8: Knit around.

Rnd 9: Knit to marker, [yo, k2tog] 4 times, knit to end of rnd.

Rnd 10: Knit around.

Rnd 11: Knit to 2 sts before marker, ssk, [k2tog, yo] 4 times, k2tog, knit to end of rnd—44 sts.

Rnd 12: Knit to 2 sts before marker, ssk, [yo, k2tog] 4 times; k2tog, knit to end of rnd—42 sts.

Rnd 13: Knit to 4 sts before marker, k2tog, ssk, remove marker, [k2tog, yo] 3 times, k2tog twice, knit to end of rnd—38 sts.

Rnd 14: K9; bind off 7 sts, k5 (including 1 st on RH needle following bind-off), then transfer last 5 sts worked to large safety pin for T-loop); bind off 6 sts; kfb, k1; transfer the 4 sts on RH needle to large safety pin (for strap); k9, then k9 from first dpn—18 sts.

Bind off all sts kwise; fasten off last st and do not cut yarn.

Strap

Transfer the st on RH needle and the 4 sts from safety pin to size 2 dpn—5 sts.

Row 1 (WS): P2tog, p1, p2tog; turn—3 sts.

Work 3-St I-Cord for 2¼ inches.

Cut yarn, leaving an 8-inch tail. Using tapestry needle, thread tail through rem sts and pull tight.

T-Loop

Transfer 5 sts from safety pin to size 2 dpn.

Row 1 (WS): Join C; p2tog, p1, p2tog, turn—3 sts.

Row 2: Ssk, k1—2 sts.

Work 2-St I-Cord for ¾ inch.

Cut yarn, leaving 8-inch tail. Using tapestry needle, thread tail through rem sts and pull tight.

Fold end of T-loop over the strap and sew securely to WS, forming a T.

Securely sew end of strap to opposite side of ankle.

Finishing

Unzip Provisional Cast-On, placing 34 live sts evenly divided on 2 smaller dpns.

Close bottom by grafting sts tog using cast-on tail and Kitchener st.

Weave in all ends.

Headband

With size 3 dpn and C, cast on 68 sts; divide sts on 3 dpns; mark beg of rnd and join, taking care not to twist sts.

Rnd 1: Work 9 sts in Seed st, pm, purl to last 9 sts, pm, work 9 sts in Seed st.

Rnds 2 and 3: Work Seed st to marker, purl to marker, work Seed st to end

Rnds 4 and 5: Work Seed st to marker, knit to marker, work Seed st to end.

Rnds 6–20: Rep [Rnds 2–5] 3 times, then work Rnds 2–4.

Rnd 21: Work 2 sts in Seed st, T1, work 4 sts in Seed st, T1, work 1 st in Seed st; knit to marker, work 4 sts in Seed st, T1, work 4 sts in Seed st.

Rnds 22 and 23: Rep Rnds 2 and 3.

Bind off pwise.

Weave in ends. ●

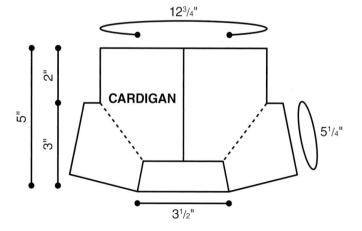

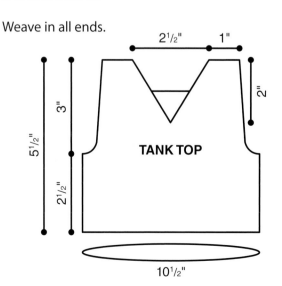

The Great Outdoors

In her cozy and colorful hoodie, walking shorts and stylish but functional boots, Amber is ready to hike the trails in the beautiful Knapp Hills.

Skill Level

 INTERMEDIATE

Finished Measurements

Hoodie chest: Approx 14 inches (buttoned)
Hoodie length to shoulder: 6¼ inches
T-shirt chest: 10 inches
T-shirt length: 5¼ inches
Shorts waist: Approx 9 inches
Shorts length: 6 inches

Materials

- Caron Simply Soft Light (DK weight; 100% acrylic; 330 yds/85g per skein): 1 skein grey #0016 (A), and small amounts pansy #0010 (B), Capri #0007 (C), bubble gum #0012 (D), honey #0003 (E) and key lime #0005 (F)

  3 LIGHT

- Size 2 (2.75mm) double-point needles
- Size 3 (3.25mm) double-point (set of 4) and 16-inch circular needle or size needed to obtain gauge
- Size 4 (3.5mm) double-point needles (set of 4)
- Size D/3 (3.25mm) crochet hook
- Stitch markers in 2 colors (A and B)
- 4 buttons

Gauge

30 sts and 40 rows/rnds = 4 inches/10 cm in St st using size 3 needles.

To save time, take time to check gauge.

Special Abbreviations

Marker A, Marker B (mA, mB): Markers in different colors (A and B)

Place marker A, place marker B (pmA, pmB): Place marker A on needle, place marker B on needle.

Slip marker (sm): Slip marker from LH to RH needle.

Lifted Increase (LI): Knit into top of st (the purl bump) in the row below next st on LH needle (see page 2).

Lifted Increase-Purl (LI-P): Purl into top of st (the purl bump) in the row below next st on LH needle.

Double yarn over (2yo): Make 2 yo's between sts.

Wrap and Turn (W&T): Slip next st pwise to RH needle. Bring yarn to RS of work between needles, then slip same st back to LH needle. Bring yarn to WS, wrapping st. Turn, leaving rem sts unworked, then beg working back in the other direction. *To hide wraps on subsequent rows:* Work to wrapped st. With RH needle, pick up wrap and work wrap tog with wrapped st (see page 2).

Pattern Stitches

Welt (worked in rounds)
Rnds 1 and 2: Purl to end.

Rnds 3 and 4: Knit to end.

Rnds 5 and 6: Purl to end.

Welt (worked in rows)
Rows 1 (RS) and 2: Knit.

Rows 3 and 4: Purl.

Rep Rows 1–4 for pat.

Stripe
Work 8 rows C, 2 rows A, 8 rows D, 2 rows A, 8 rows E, 2 rows A, 8 rows B, 2 rows A, 8 rows F.

Special Techniques
Provisional Cast-On: Using waste yarn and crochet hook, make a chain a few sts more than the number of sts to be cast on. With knitting needle and project yarn, pick up and knit in back bump of each chain until required number of cast-on sts is on needle. When indicated in pattern, "unzip" the crochet chain to free live sts (see page 4).

3-St I-Cord: Cast on 3 sts; *k3, do not turn; slip sts back to LH needle; rep from * until cord is desired length.

Pattern Notes
Hoodie body is worked in one piece from the neck down to underarm; after body is completed, hood is worked from the neck up, then sleeves are worked in the round from the yoke down.

The T-shirt is worked in the round from the bottom up; sleeves are added by casting more stitches on while working the body. If tails are woven in carefully, the "T" can be worn with either side facing out.

Shorts are worked in the round from the waist down; legs have faux pleats and are worked in the round.

Boots are worked in the round starting in the center of the sole; the sole stitches are grafted using Kitchener stitch (see page 6).

Leave 8-inch tails when joining or cutting yarns.

Hoodie

Yoke
With size 3 circular needle and A, and using Provisional Cast-On, cast on 61 sts. Do not join.

Set-up row (RS): K6 band sts, k7 left front sts, pm, k6 sleeve sts, pm, k23 back sts, pm, k6 sleeve sts, pm, k7 right front sts, k6 band sts.

Next row (WS): K6, purl to last 6 sts, k6.

Cut A and join C to beg Stripe pat.

Inc row (RS): [Knit to 1 st before marker, LI, k1, sm, LI] 4 times, knit to end—69 sts.

Maintaining first and last 6 sts in garter st for bands and working all other sts in St st and continuing Stripe pat, rep Inc row [every RS row] 15 more times, ending with a RS row—189 sts, with 6 band sts each side, 23 sts each front, 38 sts each sleeve and 55 back sts.

At the same time, work a 2-row buttonhole in right front band on 5th and 6th rows of D, B, E and F stripes as follows: On 5th row (RS): work to last 6 sts, k1, k2tog, 2yo, k2tog, k1; on 6th row (WS), k2, kfb in 2yo, work to end of row.

Division row (WS): Removing markers when you come to them, k6, *purl to 2 sts before marker, LI-P, p1, sl 1; transfer next 38 sts to waste yarn for sleeve; pass the slipped st from RH needle to LH needle; purl the slipped st and next st on LH needle tog (this helps tighten underarm gap); rep from * once, purl to last 6 sts, k6—113 body sts rem.

Body

Maintaining band sts in garter st and all other sts in St st, work Stripe pat through 7th row of F stripe, remembering to work last 2 buttonholes in B and F stripes.

Next row (WS): With F, purl across all sts. Cut F.

Designer Tip

Here is an easy way to join new colors at the end of rows. Cut the old color, leaving a 5-inch tail. Knit the first stitch of the next row (or round) with the new color, then insert the right-hand needle into the second stitch as if to knit, but before completing the stitch, bring the old yarn tail across the strand of new yarn and then knit the stitch (with the old yarn caught by the new yarn). Work the third stitch the same way but bring the new yarn's tail up and across the new yarn. This procedure "locks" the stitches, looks neater, and keeps the tails out of the way. This also works when carrying unused yarn up the wrong side of the garment.

Edging

With RS facing, join A.

Work 11 rows in Welt pat.

Bind off pwise.

Hood

Unzip Provisional Cast-On and place 61 live sts on size 3 circular needle.

With RS facing, join B.

Dec row (RS): K6, ssk, knit to last 8 sts, k2tog, k6—59 sts.

Maintaining first and last 6 sts in garter st for bands and working all other sts in St st, rep Dec row [every RS row] 6 more times, ending with a WS row—47 sts.

Inc row (RS): K6, [LI, k1] 7 times, [LI, k2] 10 times, [LI, k1] 8 times, k6; mark this row—72 sts.

Maintaining bands in garter st, work even until hood measures 4½ inches from marked Inc row, ending with a RS row.

Next row: K6, p30; transfer rem 36 sts to a dpn. Cut yarn leaving a 24-inch tail.

Working from peak of hood to bands, graft top hood sts using Kitchener st.

Sleeves

Beg at center underarm, transfer 38 sleeve sts from waste yarn to 3 size 3 dpns.

Rnd 1: Leaving a 10-inch tail, join B; pick up and knit 1 st from underarm, kfb, knit to last st, kfb, pick up and knit 1 st from underarm; pm for beg of rnd and join—42 sts.

Continue established Stripe pat through 7th row of F stripe.

Next rnd: K2tog, *k2, k2tog; rep from * around—31 sts.

Cuff

Cut F and join A.

Next rnd: [K7, k2tog] 3 times, k4—28 sts.

Work 6-rnd Welt pat.

Bind off pwise.

Finishing

Weave in ends.

Sew 4 buttons to left front band, aligned with buttonholes.

T-Shirt

With size 3 dpns and D, cast on 96 sts; divide sts evenly on 3 dpns; mark beg of rnd and join, taking care not to twist sts.

Work 25 rnds in k3, p1 rib.

Transfer last 48 sts worked to waste yarn for back—48 front sts rem.

Front

With RS facing and using Knitted Cast-On (see page 7), cast on 10 sts for left sleeve—58 sts.

Row 1 (RS): K2 (edge sts), [k3, p1] twice, work in established rib pat to end; turn and cast on 10 sts for right sleeve—68 sts.

Row 2 (WS): K2 (edge sts), [k1, p3] twice, work in established rib to last 2 sts, k2 (edge sts).

Maintaining first and last 2 sts in garter st and all other sts in established rib, work 18 rows even.

Designer Tip

This is a great way to use up leftover yarns! Make up your own color combinations. Add a matching T-shirt for each color in the hoodie.

Shape Neck

Division row (RS): Work 23 sts in established pats; join 2nd ball of yarn and bind off center 22 sts pwise; work 23 sts in established pats to end—23 sts each side.

Next row: Working both sides at once with separate balls of yarn, work even in established pats.

Dec row: Work in established pats to 4 sts before neck opening, k2tog, k2; k2, ssk, work in pats to end—22 sts each side.

Rep last 2 rows once, then work 1 WS row—21 sts each side.

Next row: Knit to 4 sts before neck opening, k2tog, k2; k2, ssk, knit to end—20 sts each side.

Transfer shoulder sts to separate holders. Cut yarn, leaving long tails.

Back

Transfer 48 sts from waste yarn to dpns.

Work same as front, but leave shoulder sts on needle.

Finishing

Graft shoulder seams using Kitchener st.

Sew underarm seam.

Weave in ends.

Shorts

Waist

With size 4 dpns and A, cast on 54 sts; divide onto 3 dpns; mark beg of rnd and join, taking care not to twist sts.

Work 6 rnds in 1x1 rib.

Inc rnd: Change to size 3 dpns; *LI, k2; rep from * to last 2 sts; LI, k1, LI, k1—82 sts.

Set-up rnd: K36 front sts, pmB, k8 left side sts, pmB, k30 back sts, pmB, k8 right side sts.

Inc rnd: Knit to 2nd marker; [LI, k2] 15 times, k8—97 sts with 45 back sts.

Knit 20 rnds.

Next rnd: Set up for front pleats as follows: k8, pmA, sl 1 for pleat, k18, pmA, sl 1 for pleat; knit to end of rnd.

Next rnd: Knit around.

Pleat rnd: [Knit to marker A, sl 1] twice, knit to end of rnd.

Rep [last 2 rnds] 4 more times.

Next rnd: Work short rows on back as follows: Knit to 5 sts before last B marker, W&T, p35, W&T, knit to end of rnd.

Next rnd: Rep Pleat rnd, hiding wraps when you come to them.

Dec rnd: Knit to 2nd B marker, [k6, k2tog] 5 times, knit to end of rnd—92 sts.

Next rnd: Rep Pleat rnd.

Next rnd: Knit.

Right Leg

Division and inc rnd: K8, sl 1, k6, [LI, k1] 3 times; keeping markers in place, transfer next 46 sts to waste yarn for left leg; LI, k28; redistribute sts on dpns as desired—50 right leg sts.

Continuing to slip "pleat st" every other rnd as established, work 10 rnds.

K21; mark this position as new beg of rnd.

Cuff

Work 6-rnd Welt pat.

Bind off pwise.

Left Leg

Beg at crotch, keeping pleat marker and removing other markers, transfer 46 left leg sts to 3 size 3 dpns.

Inc rnd: Leaving a long tail, join A; [k1, LI] 3 times, k6, sl 1, knit to last st, LI, k1—50 sts.

Continuing to slip "pleat st" every other rnd as established, work 10 rnds.

Work cuff as for right leg.

Weave in all ends.

Boots

Leaving a 15-inch tail, using size 3 dpn, Provisional Cast-On and A, cast on 32 sts.

Distribute sts on 3 dpns as follows: 9, 14, 9; mark beg of rnd and join, taking care not to twist sts.

Rnd 1: Purl around.

Rnd 2: P2, LI, p12, LI, p4, LI, p12, LI, p2—36 sts.

Rnd 3 (short rows): P25, W&T; k8, LI, k1, LI, k8, W&T; purl to end—38 sts.

Rnd 4: P3, LI, p13, LI, p6, LI, p13, LI, p3—42 sts.

Rnd 5: Purl around.

Rnd 6: P3, LI, p15, LI, p6, LI, p15, LI, p3—46 sts.

Rnd 7: P20, pm, p6, pm, p20.

Dec rnd: Knit to 2 sts before marker, ssk, k6, k2tog, knit to end of rnd—44 sts.

Working in St st, rep Dec rnd on next rnd, then [every other rnd] 5 more times—32 sts.

Next rnd: Removing markers, k6, [k2tog] 3 times, k8, [k2tog] 3 times, k6—26 sts.

Next rnd: Knit around.

Inc rnd: K3, LI, knit to last 3 sts, LI, k3—28 sts.

Rep Inc rnd [every 3 rnds] 4 times, then work 5 rnds even—36 sts.

Work 6-rnd Welt pat.

Last rnd: Bind off while dec around as follows: [p3, p2tog] 6 times, p1.

Designer Tip

Turn 7-inch or 8-inch dpns into single-point needles by securing point protectors to the back ends of the needles.

Finishing

Unzip Provisional Cast-On, placing 32 live sts evenly divided on 2 smaller dpns.

Close bottom by grafting sts tog using cast-on tail and Kitchener st.

Boot Strap

With size 2 dpns and A, work 3-St I-Cord for 1½ inches.

Sew ends across center front of boot at ankle (see photo).

Weave in all ends. ●

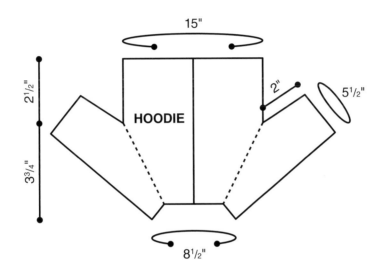

HOODIE

15"

2½"

3¾"

2"

5½"

8½"

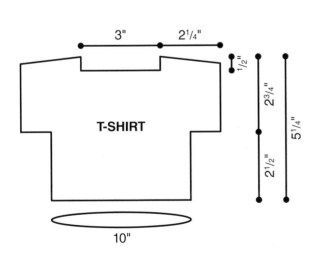

T-SHIRT

3"

2¼"

½"

2¾"

5¼"

2½"

10"

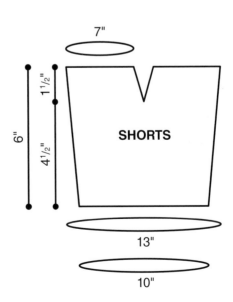

SHORTS

7"

1½"

6"

4½"

13"

10"

Back to School

Autumn is on the way and is introduced by the pumpkin and honey colors found in Sara's saucy outfit.

Skill Level

 INTERMEDIATE

Finished Measurements

Dress waist: 10½ inches
Dress length: Approx 9½ inches

Materials

- Caron Simply Soft Light (DK weight; 100% acrylic; 330 yds/85g per skein): 1 skein each pumpkin #0017 (A) and honey #0003 (B)
- Size 2 (2.75mm) double-point needles (set of 4)
- Size 3 (3.25mm) double-point (set of 4) and 16-inch circular needles or size needed to obtain gauge
- Size D/3 (3.25mm) crochet hook
- Stitch markers
- 2 large safety pins (or small stitch holders)

Gauge

30 sts and 40 rnds = 4 inches/10cm in both St st and 2-color stranded St st using larger needles.

To save time, take time to check gauge.

Special Abbreviations

Lifted Increase (LI): Knit into top of st (the purl bump) in the row below next st on LH needle (see page 2).

Lifted Increase-Purl (LI-P): Purl into top of st (the purl bump) in the row below next st on LH needle.

Slip marker (sm): Slip marker from LH needle to RH needle when you come to it.

Pattern Stitches

Seed St

Rnd 1: *K1, p1; rep from * around.

Rnd 2: Purl the knit sts and knit the purl sts.

Rep Rnd 2 for pat.

Spiral (multiple of 6 sts)

Note: A chart is provided for those preferring to work pat st from a chart.

Rnd 1: *K3, p3; rep from * around.

Rnd 2: P1, *k3, p3; rep from * to last 5 sts, k3, p2.

Rnd 3: P2, *k3, p3; rep from * to last 4 sts, k3, p1.

Rnd 4: *P3, k3; rep from * around.

Rnd 5: K1, *p3, k3; rep from * to last 5 sts, p3, k2.

Rnd 6: K2, *p3, k3; rep from * to last 4 sts, p3, k1.

Rnd 7: Rep Rnd 1.

Designer Tip

When working the pattern stitches, place a marker after each pattern repeat. This will help you keep track of where you are, and locating errors is easier. Remove the markers when they are no longer needed.

Color Patterns

See Charts A, B and C.

Special Techniques

2- or 3-St I-Cord: Cast on 2 (3) sts; *k3, do not turn; slip sts back to LH needle; rep from * until cord is desired length.

Provisional Cast-On: Using waste yarn and crochet hook, make a chain a few sts more than the number of sts to be cast on. With knitting needle and project yarn, pick up and knit in back bump of each chain until required number of cast-on sts is on needle. When indicated in pattern, "unzip" the crochet chain to free live sts (see page 4).

Pattern Notes

The dress is worked in the round from the top down.

Shoes are worked in the round starting in the center of the sole; the sole stitches are grafted using Kitchener stitch (see page 6).

All colorwork is worked using stranded 2-color method, carrying yarn not in use loosely across the wrong side (if the stranded yarn is carried too tightly, the fabric will pucker). Since stranded stockinette stitch is often tighter than one-color stockinette stitch, you may want to go up in needle size to maintain your gauge.

Dress

Neckband

With larger dpns and A, cast on 60 sts; divide sts evenly among 3 dpns; mark beg of rnd and join, taking care not to twist sts.

Work 5 rnds in Seed st.

Set-up rnd: Work in Seed st around, placing markers as follows: Work 9 sleeve sts, pm, work 26 back sts, pm, work 9 sleeve sts, pm, work 16 front sts.

Yoke

Inc rnd: [Kfb, knit to 1 st before marker, kfb, sm] 4 times around—68 sts.

Rep Inc rnd [every other rnd] 10 times, ending with an Inc rnd—148 sts.

At the same time, beg on 3rd yoke rnd, work 3-rnd Chart A, then cut B and continue with A.

Next rnd: Inc on front and back only as follows: [Knit to marker, sm, kfb, knit to 1 st before marker, kfb, sm] twice—152 sts.

Next rnd: Rep Inc rnd—160 sts.

Next rnd: Inc on sleeves and back only as follows: [Kfb, knit to 1 st before marker, kfb, sm] 3 times, knit to end of rnd—166 sts.

Next rnd: Inc on sleeves only as follows: [Kfb, knit to 1 st before marker, kfb, sm, knit to marker, sm] twice—170 sts.

Divide for Sleeves

Next rnd (dec): Removing markers when you come to them, transfer first 37 sts to waste yarn for left sleeve; k54 back sts; transfer next 37 sts to waste yarn for right sleeve; k42 front sts—96 body sts rem.

Waist

Knit 2 rnds.

Dec rnd: *[K2tog] 4 times; [k1, k2tog] 8 times; rep from * twice more—60 sts.

Work 3-rnd Chart A.

With A, knit 2 rnds.

Work 3-rnd Chart A.

With A, knit 1 rnd.

Skirt

Note: Change to circular needle when there are enough sts to do so.

Inc rnd: With A, kfb in each st around—120 sts. Cut A. Mark this rnd.

Join B; work even until skirt measures approx 2¼ inches from marked Inc rnd.

Work 3-rnd Chart B.

With B, knit 2 rnds.

Work 11-rnd Chart C.

With B, knit 2 rnds.

Work 3-rnd Chart B. Cut B.

Work 7-rnd Spiral pat.

Bind off loosely pwise.

Sleeve

Transfer 37 sleeve sts from waste yarn to 3 dpns, distributed as follows: 11, 13, 13.

Rnd 1: With A, kfb, k35, kfb; pick up and knit 1 st from body underarm—40 sts.

Work 5 rnds in Seed st.

Bind off pwise.

Finishing

Weave in all ends. Block as desired.

Socks

Note: Commercial doll shoes will not fit over these socks; the T-strap shoes that follow will stretch over the socks.

Leaving a 15-inch tail, using smaller dpn, Provisional Cast-On and B, cast on 32 sts. Divide sts on 3 dpns as follows: 9, 14, 9; mark beg of rnd and join, taking care not to twist sts

Rnds 1, 3, 5 and 7: Knit around.

Rnd 2: K2, LI, k12, LI, k4, LI, k12, LI, k2—36 sts.

Rnd 4: K4, LI, k12, L, k4, LI, k12, LI, k4—40 sts.

Rnd 6: K3, LI, k15, LI, k4, L, k15, LI, k3—44 sts.

Rnd 8: K19, pm, k6, pm, k19.

Dec rnd: Slipping markers when you come to them, knit to 2 sts before marker, ssk, k6, k2tog, knit to end of rnd—42 sts.

Rep Dec rnd [every other rnd] 5 more times—32 sts.

Next rnd: Removing markers, k6, [k2tog] 3 times, k8, [k2tog] 3 times, k6—26 sts.

Knit 2 rnds.

Next rnd: [K3, LI] 8 times, k2—34 sts.

Work 7 rnds in 1x1 rib.

Join A; knit 1 rnd.

Work 1 rnd in 1x1 rib. Cut A, leaving an 8-inch tail.

With B, knit 1 rnd.

Work 2 rnds in 1x1 rib.

Bind off loosely in rib. Cut B, leaving an 8-inch tail.

Finishing

Unzip Provisional Cast-On, placing 34 live sts evenly divided on 2 smaller dpns.

Close bottom by grafting sts tog using cast-on tail and Kitchener st.

Weave in all ends.

T-Strap Shoes

Leaving a 15-inch tail, using smaller dpn, Provisional Cast-On and A, cast on 34 sts. Distribute sts on 3 dpns as follows: 10, 14, 10; mark beg of rnd and join, taking care not to twist sts.

Rnds 1, 3, 5, 7, 8 and 9: Knit around.

Rnd 2: K3, LI, k11, LI, k6, LI, k11, LI, k3—38 sts.

Rnd 4 (inc): K3, LI, k13, LI, k6, LI, k13, LI, k3—42 sts.

Rnd 6 (inc): K3, LI, k15, LI, k6, LI, k15, LI, k3—46 sts.

Rnd 10: K19, pm, k8, k19.

Rnds 11 and 12: Knit to 2 sts before marker, ssk, k8, k2tog, knit to end of rnd—42 sts at end of Rnd 12.

Rnd 13: Knit to 4 sts before marker, k2tog, ssk, remove marker, k8, [k2tog] twice, knit to end of rnd—38 sts.

Rnd 14: K9; bind off 7 sts, k5 (including 1 st on RH needle following bind-off), then transfer last 5 sts worked to large safety pin for T-loop); bind off 6 sts; kfb, k1; transfer the 4 sts on RH needle to large safety pin (for strap); k9, then k9 from first needle—18 sts.

Bind off all sts kwise; fasten off last st and do not cut yarn.

Strap

Transfer the st on RH needle and the 4 sts from safety pin to smaller dpn—5 sts.

Row 1 (WS): P2tog, p1, p2tog; turn—3 sts.

Work 3-St I-Cord for 2¼ inches.

Cut yarn, leaving an 8-inch tail. Using tapestry needle, thread tail through rem sts and pull tight.

T-Loop

Transfer 5 sts from safety pin to smaller dpn.

Row 1 (WS): Join A; p2tog, p1, p2tog, turn—3 sts.

Row 2: Ssk, k1—2 sts.

Work 2-St I-Cord for ¾ inch.

Cut yarn leaving 8-inch tail. Using tapestry needle, thread tail through rem sts and pull tight.

Finishing

Fold end of T-loop over the strap and sew securely to WS, forming a T.

Securely sew end of strap to opposite side of ankle.

Unzip Provisional Cast-On, placing 34 live sts evenly divided on 2 smaller dpns.

Close bottom by grafting sts tog using cast-on tail and Kitchener st.

Weave in all ends.

Headband

With larger dpns and A, cast on 66 sts. Divide sts evenly on 3 dpns; mark beg of rnd and join, taking care not to twist sts.

Work 5 rnds in Seed st.

Work 3-rnd Chart A.

With A, knit 4 rnds.

Work 3-rnd Chart A. Cut B.

With A, knit 1 rnd.

Work 5 rnds in Seed st.

Bind off in pat.

Weave in ends. ●

CHART A   **CHART B**

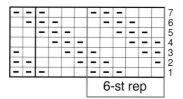

STITCH KEY

☐	K
−	P

SPIRAL PAT CHART

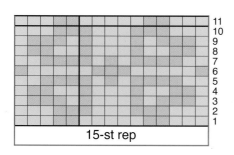

15-st rep

CHART C

COLOR KEY

	A
	B

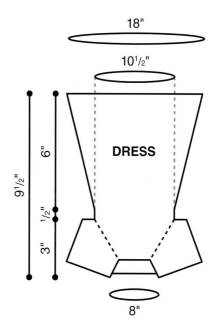

DRESS

Snow Day

Racing down snow covered hills in her Fair Isle
outfit, Ronnie does not mind the cold!

Skill Level

■■■□ EXPERIENCED

Finished Measurements

Sweater chest circumference: 12 inches
Sweater length: 6¾ inches
Pants waist: 10 inches
Pants length: 10 inches
Hat circumference: 10½ inches

Materials

- Caron Simply Soft Light
  (DK weight; 100% acrylic;
  330 yds/85g per skein): 1 skein
  each Capri #0007 (A), Hawaiian sky #0009 (B)
  and heavy cream #0002 (C)
- Patons Moxie (eyelash yarn; 100% polyester;
  96 yds/100g per ball): 1 ball lynx #81008 (D)
- Size 3 (3.25mm) double-point (set of 4) and
  16-inch circular needles or size needed to
  obtain gauge
- Size 4 (3.5mm) double-point needles (set of 4)
- Size D/3 (3.25mm) crochet hook
- Stitch markers in 2 colors (A and B)
- Fiberfill (optional)

3 LIGHT

Gauge

30 sts and 40 rnds = 4 inches/10 cm in stranded
2-color St st with smaller needles.

To save time, take time to check gauge.

Special Abbreviations

Marker A, Marker B (mA, mB): Markers in different
colors (A and B)

Place marker A, place marker B (pmA, pmB): Place
marker A on needle, place marker B on needle.

Lifted Increase (LI): Knit into top of st (the purl
bump) in the row below next st on LH needle
(see page 2).

Wrap and Turn (W&T): Slip next st pwise to RH
needle. Bring yarn to RS of work between needles,
then slip same st back to LH needle. Bring yarn to
WS, wrapping st. Turn, leaving rem sts unworked,
then beg working back in the other direction. *To hide
wraps on subsequent rows:* Work to wrapped st. With
RH needle, pick up wrap and work wrap tog with
wrapped st (see page 2).

Slip marker (sm): Slip marker when you come to it.

Pattern Stitches

Seed St

Rnd 1: *K1, p1; rep from * around.

Rnd 2: Purl the knit sts and knit the purl sts.

Rep Rnd 2 for pat.

Color Patterns

See Charts A, B and C.

Special Technique

Provisional Cast-On: Using waste yarn and crochet hook, make a chain a few sts more than the number of sts to be cast on. With knitting needle and project yarn, pick up and knit in back bump of each chain until required number of cast-on sts is on needle. When indicated in pattern, "unzip" the crochet chain to free live sts (see page 4).

Pattern Notes

Sweater is worked in the round from the neck down; after yoke is complete, body and sleeves are worked separately.

Pants are worked in the round from the waist down, ending with the stirrups; legs have faux pleats; short rows in the back allow needed fullness.

Hat is worked in the round from the bottom up; pompom is a stuffed ball.

Boots are worked in the round starting in the center of the sole; the sole stitches are grafted using Kitchener stitch (see page 6).

All colorwork is worked using stranded 2-color method, carrying yarn not-in-use loosely across the wrong side (if the stranded yarn is carried tightly, the fabric will pucker). Since stranded stockinette stitch is often tighter than one-color stockinette stitch, you may want to go up in needle size to maintain your gauge.

Each boot uses approximately 4 yards of eyelash yarn. When working with the eyelash yarn, cut off about half the eyelashes, or as desired, to make the yarn more manageable.

Sweater

Collar

With larger dpns and A, cast on 52 sts; divide sts on 3 dpns as follows: 18, 18, 16; mark beg of rnd and join, taking care not to twist sts.

Knit 5 rnds.

Next rnd: Change to smaller dpns and B; knit around.

Yoke

Raglan set-up rnd: K7 sleeve sts, pm, k24 back sts, pm, k7 sleeve sts, pm, k14 front sts.

Inc rnd: [Kfb, knit to 1 st before marker, kfb, sm] 4 times around—60 sts.

Rep Inc rnd [every other rnd] 14 times—172 sts.

At the same time, beg with first Inc rnd, work 10-rnd Chart A; then work 15-rnd Chart B, referring to separate charts for positions of snowflake motifs on sleeves, back and front; then rep Rnds 6–10 of Chart A.

Division rnd: Transfer first 37 sts to waste yarn for sleeve; with B, k54 back sts; transfer next 37 sts to waste yarn for sleeve; kfb, knit to last st, kfb—100 body sts rem.

Body

Work even, continuing stripe pat as follows: Work Rnds 2–10 of Chart A, then work Rnds 1–9.

Designer Tip

When working in the round on three double-point needles, attach and leave a small safety pin in the fabric between the first and third needles to alert you to the end of the round (markers fall off so easily).

Next 3 rnds: *K2 B, k2 A; rep from * around.

Next 3 rnds: *K2 A, k2 B; rep from * around.

Next 3 rnds: *K2 B, k2 A; rep from * around. Cut B.

Work 3 rnds in Seed st.

Bind off in pat.

Sleeves

Transfer 37 sleeve sts from waste yarn to smaller dpns; divide sts on dpns as follows: 11, 15, 11.

Rnd 1: Join B; kfb, k35, kfb; pick up and knit 1 st from body underarm—40 sts.

Work even, continuing stripe pat as follows: Work Rnds 2–10 of Chart A, then work Rnds 1–7.

Next 2 rnds: *K2 B, k2 A; rep from * around.

Next 2 rnds: *K2 A, k2 B; rep from * around.

Next 2 rnds: *K2 B, k2 A; rep from * around. Cut B.

Dec rnd: With A, k4, [k2tog, k4] 6 times around—34 sts.

Knit 10 rnds.

Bind off.

Finishing

Weave in all ends.

Pants

Waist

With larger dpns and B, cast on 54 sts; divide sts on 3 dpns; mark beg of rnd and join, taking care not to twist sts.

Work 6 rnds in 1x1 rib.

Inc rnd: Change to smaller dpns; *LI, k2; rep from * to last 2 sts; LI, k1, LI, k1—82 sts.

Set-up rnd: K36 front sts, pmB, k8 left side sts, pmB, k30 back sts, pmB, k8 right side sts.

Inc rnd: Slipping markers when you come to them, k44, [LI, k2] 15 times across back sts; k8—97 sts with 45 back sts.

Knit 20 rnds.

Next rnd: Set up for front pleats as follows: K8, pmA, sl 1 for pleat, k18, k9, pmA, sl 1 for pleat, knit to end of rnd.

Next rnd: Knit.

Pleat rnd: [Knit to mA, sl 1] twice, knit to end of rnd.

Rep [last 2 rnds] 4 times.

Next rnd: Work short rows on back as follows: Knit to 5 sts before 3rd B marker, W&T, p35, W&T, knit to end of rnd.

Next rnd: Rep Pleat rnd, hiding wraps when you come to them.

Dec rnd: Knit to 2nd B marker, [k6, k2tog] 5 times, knit to end of rnd—92 sts.

Next rnd: Rep Pleat rnd.

Knit 1 rnd.

Division rnd: K8, sl 1, k6, [LI, k1] 3 times; keeping pleat marker in place, transfer next 46 sts to waste yarn for left leg; knit to end of rnd—49 sts. Redistribute sts on 3 dpns as follows: 21-15-13.

Right Leg

Maintain established pleat pat, continuing to slip pleat st every other rnd.

At the same time, shape leg as follows:

Work 6 rnds even.

Dec Rnd 1: Work to last 2 sts on Needle 1, k2tog; knit to end of rnd—48 sts.

Rep last 7 rnds once, then work 6 rnds even—47 sts.

Dec Rnd 2: Work across Needle 1; k2tog, knit to end of rnd—46 sts.

Rep Dec Rnd 2 [every 4 rnds] 5 times—41 sts.

Work 3 rnds even, then work Dec Rnd 1—40 sts.

Work 2 rnds even, then work Dec Rnd 2—39 sts.

Work 2 rnds even.

Next rnd: Removing marker, k8, *[kfb] 6 times, then transfer the 6 sts that were worked tbl to a small safety pin and let it hang in front* (these sts will be for the stirrups); k7, k2tog, k7; rep from * to *—38 sts on dpns.

Bind off rem sts pwise.

Stirrups

With RS facing, transfer one set of 6 sts to smaller dpn.

Join B; work 15 rows in St st.

Transfer other set of 6 sts to smaller dpn.

Graft both sides of stirrup tog using Kitchener st.

Left Leg

Transfer the 46 sts from waste yarn to 3 smaller dpns, distributed as follows (counting from crotch): 18, 15, 13.

Inc rnd: Leaving a long tail, join B; [LI, k1] twice, LI, k7; sl 1, knit to end of round—49 sts.

Maintain established pleat pat, continuing to slip pleat st every other rnd.

At the same time, shape leg as follows:

Work 6 rnds even.

Dec Rnd 1: K2tog, knit to end of rnd—48 sts.

Work 6 rnds even.

Dec Rnd 2: Knit to last 2 sts, k2tog—47 sts.

Continuing to alternate Dec Rnds 1 and 2, dec 1 st [every 6 rnds] once, then [every 4 rnds] 6 times—40 sts.

Work 2 rnds even, then work Dec Rnd 2—39 sts.

Work 2 rnds even.

Complete left leg and stirrup as for right leg.

Boots

Leaving a 15-inch tail, using smaller dpns, Provisional Cast-On and C, cast on 32 sts; divide sts as follows: 9, 14, 9; mark beg of rnd and join, taking care not to twist sts.

Rnd 1: Purl.

Rnd 2: P2, LI, p12, LI, p4, LI, p12, LI, p2—36 sts.

Rnd 3 (with short rows): P25, W&T; k8, LI, k1, LI, k8, W&T; purl to end—38 sts.

Rnd 4: P3, LI, p13, LI, p6, LI, p13, LI, p3—42 sts.

Rnd 6: Purl.

Rnd 7: P3, LI, p15, LI, p6, LI, p15, LI, p3—46 sts.

Rnd 9: P20, pm, p6, pm, p20.

Dec rnd: Knit to 2 sts before marker, ssk, k6, k2tog, knit to end—44 sts.

Working in St st, rep Dec rnd on next rnd, then [every other rnd] 5 times, ending with a plain rnd—32 sts.

Next rnd: Removing markers, k6, [k2tog] 3 times, k8, [k2tog] 3 times, k6—26 sts.

Knit 2 rnds.

Next rnd: [K3, LI] 8 times, k2—34 sts.

Knit 7 rnds. Cut C.

Fur Top

Note: *If not using eyelash yarn, work last 4 rnds in Seed st with C, binding off in pat.*

Join D; knit 4 rnds.

Bind off.

Finishing

Unzip Provisional Cast-On, placing 34 live sts evenly divided on 2 smaller dpns.

Close bottom by grafting sts tog using cast-on tail and Kitchener st.

Weave in all ends.

Designer Tip

When putting the boots on the doll, slip a table knife between the boot and pant leg after the boot is on to smooth the pant leg.

Hat

With smaller dpns and B, cast on 66 sts; divide sts evenly on 3 dpns; mark beg of rnd and join, taking care not to twist sts.

Rnds 1–5: Work 1x1 rib.

Rnd 6: Join A; k20, LI, k20, LI, knit to end—68 sts.

Rnds 7 and 8: *K2 B, k2 A; rep from * around.

Rnds 9 and 10: *K2 A, k2 B; rep from * around.

Rnds 11 and 12: Rep Rnd 7; cut A.

Rnds 13 and 14: With B, knit around.

Rnd 15: K20, LI, k20, LI, knit to end—70 sts.

Rnds 16–24: With B and C, work [Chart C] 10 times around; if desired, pm between reps. Cut C.

Rnds 25 and 26: With B, knit around.

Rnds 27 and 28: Join A; knit around.

Rnd 29: *K1B, k1A; rep from * around.

Rnd 30: With A, knit around.

Shape Crown

Rnd 1: With A, [k3, k2tog] 14 times—56 sts.

Rnds 2 and 3: With B, knit around.

Rnd 4: [K2, k2tog] 14 times—42 sts.

Rnd 5: *K1 A, k1 B; rep from * around. Cut A.

Rnds 6 and 8: With B, knit around.

Rnd 7: K2tog around—21 sts.

Rnd 9: [K2tog] 10 times, k1—11 sts.

Rnd 10: [K2tog] 5 times, k1—6 sts.

Pompom

Rnd 1: Kfb in each st around—12 sts.

Rnd 2: Kfb in each st around—24 sts.

Rnds 3–10: Work in Seed st.

Rnd 11: K2tog around—12 sts.

Rnd 12: [K2tog] 4 times; stuff pompom with fiberfill or with scraps of B (which won't show color through spaces in sts); [k2tog] twice—6 sts.

Cut yarn, leaving a 15-inch tail.

Using tapestry needle, thread tail through rem sts, and pull tight. Bring tail through to bottom of pompom and wind tail around base of pompom so stuffing doesn't work itself out of pompom. If desired, tack outer base of pompom to top of hat.

Weave in all ends.

Mittens

With smaller dpn and C, cast on 22 sts; divide on 3 dpns as follows: 8-6-8; mark beg of rnd and join, taking care not to twist sts.

Work 7 rnds in 1x1 rib.

Inc rnd: [LI, k4] 5 times, LI, k2—28 sts.

Knit 5 rnds.

Thumbhole rnd: K1; using waste yarn, k5, then pass those 5 sts back to LH needle; using working yarn, knit those 5 sts again, then knit to end of rnd.

Knit 11 rnds.

Dec rnd: [K2tog, k2] 6 times, [k2tog] twice—20 sts.

Next rnd: K2tog around—10 sts.

Cut yarn, leaving a 12-inch tail.

Divide sts on 2 dpns (5 on each).

Close top by grafting sts tog using Kitchener st.

Thumb

Carefully remove waste yarn from the 5 sts, transferring the top and bottom loops to 2 dpns as you go—11 sts. Divide sts on 3 dpns and mark beg of rnd.

Leaving a long tail, join C.

Knit 5 rnds.

Dec rnd: [K2tog] 5 times, k1—6 sts.

Divide sts on 2 dpns (3 on each).

Close top by grafting sts tog using Kitchener st.

Close gaps around the thumb base.

Weave in all ends. ●

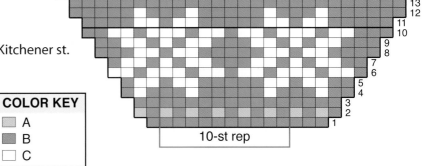

CHART B: FRONT

COLOR KEY
- A
- B
- C

CHART B: BACK

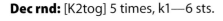

CHART A

CHART C

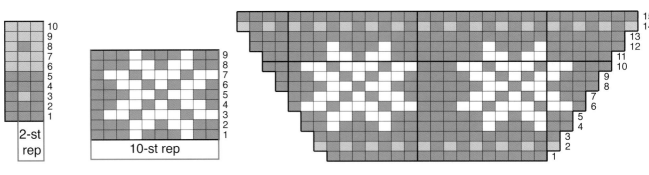

CHART B: SLEEVES

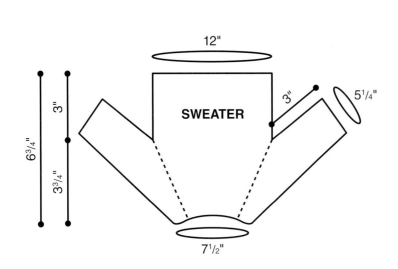

12"

SWEATER

3"

5¼"

6¾"

3"

3¾"

7½"

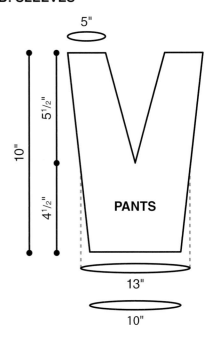

5"

5½"

10"

4½"

PANTS

13"

10"

Meet the Designer

In addition to an obsession with knitting, Jeanne has taught the medical secretarial program at a Minnesota technical college, worked as a copy editor/secretary at a Wisconsin university, and enjoyed a 28-year theater career, performing in over 60 stage productions. Her terraced perennial flower garden has been a labor of love for 20 years. Her four children have long left home to raise families of their own. Jeanne and her husband of 53 years, Harlyn, live in Wisconsin with their canine friend, Lotsa Moola.

Special Thanks

Special thanks to Spinrite for supplying all of the wonderful yarn for this book. All of the outfits were made with Caron Simply Soft Light and Patons Moxie.

Spinrite
320 Livingstone Ave. S. Box 40
Listowel, ON
Canada
N4W 3H3

Knitting Needle Conversion Chart

U.S.	1	2	3	4	5	6	7	8	9	10	10½	11	13	15	17	19	35
Continental-mm	2.25	2.75	3.25	3.5	3.75	4	4.5	5	5.5	6	6.5	8	9	10	12	15	19

Inches Into Millimetres & Centimetres

All measurements are rounded off slightly.

inches	mm	cm	inches	cm	inches	cm	inches	cm	inches	cm
⅛	3	0.3	3	7.5	13	33.0	26	66.0	39	99.0
¼	6	0.6	3½	9.0	14	35.5	27	68.5	40	101.5
⅜	10	1.0	4	10.0	15	38.0	28	71.0	41	104.0
½	13	1.3	4½	11.5	16	40.5	29	73.5	42	106.5
⅝	15	1.5	5	12.5	17	43.0	30	76.0	43	109.0
¾	20	2.0	5½	14	18	46.0	31	79.0	44	112.0
⅞	22	2.2	6	15.0	19	48.5	32	81.5	45	114.5
1	25	2.5	7	18.0	20	51.0	33	84.0	46	117.0
1¼	32	3.8	8	20.5	21	53.5	34	86.5	47	119.5
1½	38	3.8	9	23.0	22	56.0	35	89.0	48	122.0
1¾	45	4.5	10	25.5	23	58.5	36	91.5	49	124.5
2	50	5.0	11	28.0	24	61.0	37	94.0	50	127.0
2½	65	6.5	12	30.5	25	63.5	38	96.5		

Knitting Basics

Need help? ▶ **StitchGuide.com** • ILLUSTRATED GUIDES • HOW-TO VIDEOS

Long-Tail Cast-On

Make a slip knot on the right needle.

Place the thumb and index finger of your left hand between the yarn ends with the long yarn end over your thumb, and the strand from the yarn ball over your index finger. Close your other fingers over the strands to hold them against your palm. Spread your thumb and index fingers apart and draw the yarn into a "V."

Place the needle in front of the strand around your thumb and bring it underneath this strand. Carry the needle over and under the strand on your index finger.

Draw the strand through the loop on your thumb. Drop the loop from your thumb and draw up the strand to form a stitch on the knitting needle.

Repeat until you have cast on the number of stitches indicated in the pattern.

Knit (k)

With yarn in back, insert the right needle from front to back into the next stitch on the left needle.

Bring the yarn under and over the right needle, wrapping the yarn counterclockwise around the needle.

Use the right needle to pull the loop through the stitch.

Slide the stitch off the left needle.

Purl (p)

With yarn in front, insert the right needle from back to front into the next stitch on the left needle.

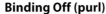

Wrap the yarn counterclockwise around the right needle.

Use the right needle to pull the loop through the stitch and to the back.

Slide the stitch off left needle.

Bind Off

Binding Off (knit)

Knit the first two stitches on the left needle. Insert the left needle into the first stitch worked on the right needle, then lift that first stitch over the second stitch and off the right needle. Knit the next stitch and repeat.

When one stitch remains on the right needle, cut the yarn and draw the tail through the last stitch to fasten off.

Binding Off (purl)

Purl the first two stitches on the left needle.

Insert the left needle into the first stitch worked on the right needle, then lift the first stitch over the second stitch and off the right needle. Purl the next stitch and repeat.

When one stitch remains on the right needle, cut the yarn and draw the tail through the last stitch to fasten off.

Increase (inc)

Bar Increase (knit: kfb)

Knit the next stitch but do not remove the original stitch from the left needle.

Insert the right needle behind the left needle and knit into the back of the same stitch.

Slip the original stitch off the left needle.

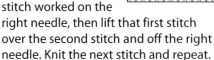

Bar Increase (purl: pfb)

Purl the next stitch but do not remove the original stitch from the left needle.

Insert the right needle behind the left needle and purl into the back of the same stitch.

Slip the original stitch off the left needle.

Make 1 With Left Twist (M1L)

Insert the left needle from front to back under the strand that runs between the stitch on the right needle and the stitch on the left needle.

With the right needle, knit into the back of the loop on the left needle.

To make this increase on the purl side, insert left needle in same manner and purl into the back of the loop.

Make 1 With Right Twist (M1R)

Insert the left needle from back to front under the strand that runs between the stitch on the right needle and the stitch on the left needle.

With the right needle, knit into the front of the loop on the left needle.

To make this increase on the purl side, insert left needle in same manner and purl into the front of the loop.

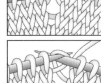

Make 1 With Backward Loop

Use your thumb to make a backward loop of yarn over the right needle. Slip the loop from your thumb onto the needle and pull to tighten.

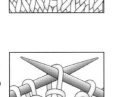
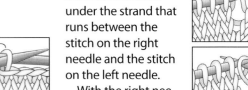
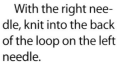

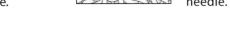

Decrease (dec)

Knit 2 Together (k2tog)

Insert the right needle through the next two stitches on the left needle as if to knit. Knit these two stitches together as one.

Purl 2 Together (p2tog)

Insert the right needle through the next two stitches on the left needle as if to purl. Purl these two stitches together as one.

Slip, Slip, Knit (ssk)

Slip the next two stitches, one at a time, from the left needle to the right needle as if to knit.

Insert the left needle through both slipped stitches in front of the right needle.

Knit these two stitches together.

Slip, Slip, Purl (ssp)

Slip the next two stitches, one at a time, from the left needle to the right needle as if to knit.

Slip these stitches back to the left needle keeping them twisted.

Purl these two stitch-es together through their back loops.

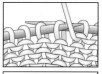

Standard Abbreviations

[ ] work instructions within brackets as many times as directed

( ) work instructions within parentheses in the place directed

** repeat instructions following the asterisks as directed

* repeat instructions following the single asterisk as directed

" inch(es)

approx approximately

beg begin/begins/beginning

CC contrasting color

ch chain stitch

cm centimeter(s)

cn cable needle

dec(s) decrease/decreases/ decreasing

dpn(s) double-point needle(s)

g gram(s)

inc(s) increase/increases/ increasing

k knit

k2tog knit 2 stitches together

kfb knit in front and back

kwise knitwise

LH left hand

m meter(s)

MC main color

mm millimeter(s)

oz ounce(s)

p purl

p2tog purl 2 stitches together

pat(s) pattern(s)

pm place marker

psso pass slipped stitch over

pwise purlwise

rem remain/remains/ remaining

rep(s) repeat(s)

rev St st reverse stockinette stitch

RH right hand

rnd(s) rounds

RS right side

skp slip 1 knitwise, knit 1, pass slipped stitch over—a left-leaning decrease

sk2p slip 1 knitwise, knit 2 together, pass slipped stitch over the stitch from the knit-2-together decrease—a left-leaning double decrease

sl slip

sl 1 kwise slip 1 knitwise

sl 1 pwise slip 1 purlwise

sl st(s) slipped stitch(es)

ssk slip 2 stitches, 1 at a time, knitwise; knit these stitch-es together through the back loops—a left-leaning decrease

st(s) stitch(es)

St st stockinette stitch

tbl through back loop(s)

tog together

WS wrong side

wyib with yarn in back

wyif with yarn in front

yd(s) yard(s)

yfwd yarn forward

yo (yo's) yarn over(s)

Standard Yarn Weight System

Categories of yarn, gauge ranges, and recommended needle sizes

Yarn Weight Symbol & Category Names	0 LACE	1 SUPER FINE	2 FINE	3 LIGHT	4 MEDIUM	5 BULKY	6 SUPER BULKY
Type of Yarns in Category	Fingering, 10-Count Crochet Thread	Sock, Fingering, Baby	Sport, Baby	DK, Light Worsted	Worsted, Afghan, Aran	Chunky, Craft, Rug	Bulky, Roving
Knit Gauge Range* in Stockinette Stitch to 4 inches	33–40 sts**	27–32 sts	23–26 sts	21–24 sts	16–20 sts	12–15 sts	6–11 sts
Recommended Needle in Metric Size Range	1.5–2.25mm	2.25–3.25mm	3.25–3.75mm	3.75–4.5mm	4.5–5.5mm	5.5–8mm	8mm and larger
Recommended Needle U.S. Size Range	000 to 1	1 to 3	3 to 5	5 to 7	7 to 9	9 to 11	11 and larger

* GUIDELINES ONLY: The above reflect the most commonly used gauges and needle sizes for specific yarn categories.
** Lace weight yarns are often knitted on larger needles and hooks to create lacy, openwork patterns. Accordingly, a gauge range is difficult to determine. Always follow the gauge stated in your pattern.

Skill Levels

BEGINNER

Beginner projects for first-time knitters using basic stitches. Minimal shaping.

EASY

Easy projects using basic stitches, repetitive stitch patterns, simple color changes, and simple shaping and finishing.

INTERMEDIATE

Intermediate projects with a variety of stitches, mid-level shaping and finishing.

EXPERIENCED

Experienced projects using advanced techniques and stitches, detailed shaping and refined finishing.

Photo Index

2

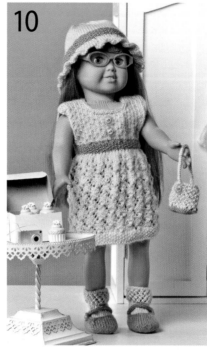

10

17

24

32

38

Annie's

Sassy Knit Outfits for 18-Inch Dolls is published by Annie's, 306 East Parr Road, Berne, IN 46711. Printed in USA. Copyright © 2014 Annie's. All rights reserved. This publication may not be reproduced in part or in whole without written permission from the publisher.

RETAIL STORES: If you would like to carry this pattern book or any other Annie's publications, visit AnniesWSL.com.

Every effort has been made to ensure that the instructions in this pattern book are complete and accurate. We cannot, however, take responsibility for human error, typographical mistakes or variations in individual work. Please visit AnniesCustomerCare.com to check for pattern updates.

978-1-59635-974-1

1 2 3 4 5 6 7 8 9